Carmen Martins

The Hatch Family

THE

RICH

FAMILY

Once upon a time, a long time ago, in the middle of the woods, on the top of a hill, lived the Rich FAMILY.

PENNY was a little girl who was in grade ONE. Her hobby was collecting leaves. PENNIE'S favorite leaf was the MAPLE LEAF.

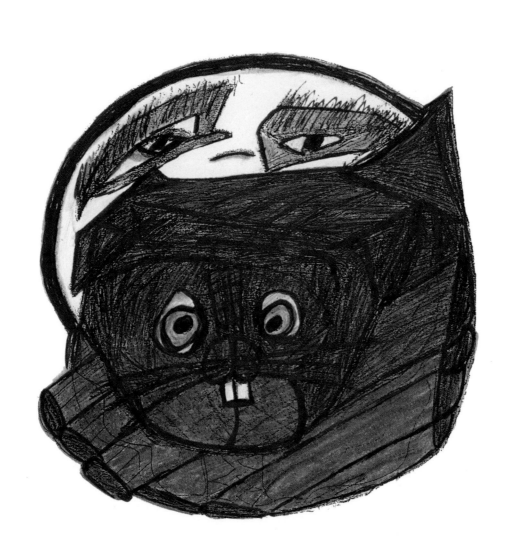

NICKEL was PENNIE'S sister.
NICKEL was in grade FIVE.
NICKEL enjoyed reading books.
Especially books about BEAVERS.

DIME was Penny and Nickel's brother. DIME was in high school in grade TEN. DIME always dreamed about going on a long voyage on the ship called, 'THE BLUE NOSE.'

QUARTER was their older brother.
He was in college. QUARTER was
TWENTY-FIVE years old. QUARTER
enjoyed hunting.
Especially hunting CARIBOO.

LOONIE was mother. LOONIE was number ONE at home. She kept an eye on her family just like a bird. LOONIE was as pretty as a LOON.

TOONIE was father. TOONIE was number TWO at home. He always listened to mother. TOONIE was like a BIG cuddly WHITE POLAR BEAR.

LOONIE and TOONIE constantly reminded their children. 'YOU ARE very VALUABLE and YOU WILL ALWAYS be a PART of US.' 'REMEMBER, one day YOU will ADD UP to be a LOONIE or TOONIE.'